Also by Enza Marie Putignano

Deep Low Bow
Poems & Stories
of Impermanence & Love

Soft Downward Eyes
Poems & Stories of
Cosmic Remembrance

By
Enza Marie
Putignano

"I believe in everything;
nothing is sacred.
I believe in nothing;
everything is sacred.
Ha Ha Ho Ho Hee Hee."

~ Tom Robbins,
Even Cowgirls Get the Blues

(Halo)

Let us go to the sea,
return to our remembering.
We, the streaming of stardust, the
splitting of cells. Golden mean of
our being riding waves eternal.
Ascending to fall.
Swell.
Rise again.
So we may empty our lungs,
guts, minds. One more,
one-more-time.
Contact.
Always contact.
Merging flat-steady.
Rocks transform with
recognition. Observer
observed. We shift.
Neolithic.
Re-patterning our innermost sun
with a wide-open concentric kiss.
Circles skipping squares
to triangulate.
Winking our third eye.
We, the hollows,
spiraling deeply home.
Holding gentle
inward hands
to return
heads bowed low
with lunar know.
Holy darkness held close.
We submerge.
We return.

(Saved You a Seat)

I cleared a place for you at the table
this morning, never mind the jack
hammers and constant buzz of
generators. Rattle axel
cobblestone holes.
There is great peace
here within
our bowls.

And
I made ginger tea, too,
so we may feel the pleasant
fire of our highest churning.
As together we slide full
silver spoons beneath
each morsel of "Yes"
to carry what's
already ours
deeper
deeper
deeper
down.

(Next Move)

All of this has to go.
Sinking thick animal furs,
comfort of cover and heat,
crisp vintage plates,
delicate stacking
of gold-trimmed meals.
Red leather straps
buckling
the crux of the world
at my ankle.
Crash of cymbals brass,
and boom of stretching skin.
All of it
has
to
go.
Rainbow obsidian
altar of my heart,
and tears, carnelian.
Ten thousand petals
open
for a time
to settle
above the dust of us.

All of this
has
to
go.
But where?

If I were a black shiny crow
I would know.

(Our Nucleus)

On my way to the no show I stopped to pick a dandelion and tuck it behind my left ear. Later, I was surprised crossing the boulevard at the corner of Joe's Doughnut Shop, to hear a song, thin at first, coming through from above. It was difficult to really hear the words for they were in a language I knew, but didn't understand.

When I pressed my right ear, closing off the sounds of early morning dynamite, Earth's tired contraction, the whiz of revving-red anxiety, stop lights and smog, I could hear a drum. Ancient beat of blood and heart's churning, 300,000 light years known, drawing my body in, up, down, In. Up. Down.

Brown-orange ants were there, busy with purpose. Their green shields of mighty-might and clarity deflecting light from above. Onward. Below. Their steadfast focus and connection leading them always home. Ants were there, and seeds, too, round, dry and the color of closing winter. The wind rolling them long to thin-rivers snaking the curb. I did not step on them. I sat down. Listening below. This language from above. Pressing my right ear.

The dandelion turned her head and sighed. It seems the story told is an old one. One she's heard many times before. In her exhale every word. Every word ever all at once flowing the gutter by the doughnut shop, tickling the souls of humanity, sparking a game of hopscotch. The pause of a tossed rock. Onward spinning home.

Snaking seeds, yeasty grow and the thinness of the song carrying on, bright yellow, lifting the smog of uncertainty to cirrus clouds of hope, high crystals wrapping an early morning face with comfort and calm. Deep inhale and release. The smell of hot coffee.

This flower. This seed. No longer the smog that will not breathe. We clear to transform our block of traffic, our persona, our edge, to a mind field of neutral flame, to reels of soft molecules colliding, exchanging, without direction, without thought. Cream filling.

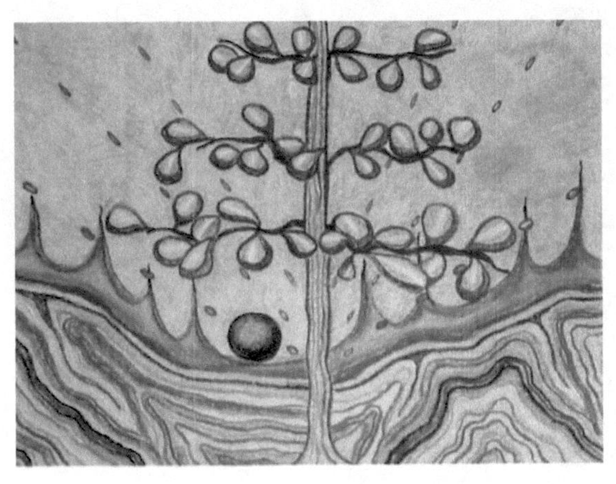

(In the Wake Of)

Dear Patience,

Could you close the door, please?
The ocean floor swept through here
this morning and I'm hoping for
a few pearls for breakfast,
though one will do. Chalky
half-shell, open, unhinged.
The two of us. Something
precious starting out.

Bottom feeders waving
through, capturing the perfect
irritant of you. And time, golden,
lodged under tenderness and the
shedding of skin. Soft cool skin.

Seahorse questions wrapping
round and lifting up.

Bio-luminescence.

Endless waves calling, a-buzz
of mañana song.

Yeah really please.
I need you,
Dear Patience,
I need you to close
the door please on your
way out. Leave your slow
steady
rise
behind.

(Considering What Floats)

If I asked you to water my late summer garden
for a while, to leave the weeds and the slugs,
to simply open the taps of our good intentions,
of our memories of our first ever rainbow atop
Mt. Holyguard and the three-legged dog, who
visited your grandmother's lakeside cottage,
crawling to you, deep under measure, to cool
terrestrial holes, to aiming-a-hose holes, to quietly
going-nowhere-going-everywhere holes. Three
determined legs leading a warm beating body
to your receiving, tiny green snakes and
chipmunks curled at your feet. You,
then, waking today, to spray all
possibility, sparkle-drop mist,
and puddles forming, sinking
in, forming, sinking in....
Would you,
if I asked,
would you
say, "Yes"?

(Clockwise)

Crusty dishes piled high,
resting all day in a dirty
stainless pit. Coffee grinds
and carrot peelings mixing
with oil, soap, water.
Small mountain of life.
And again, it is
time to chop.
Wooden block.
To cleave straight
to the heart. One
sure stroke
seeking
balm within.
Smooth cool skin.
Bright firm flesh,
and fresh. To be
transformed
with heat
and attention.
Cinnamon,
cardamom,
clove. Slender green
stalks cut off from tough
gray roots. Tender budding
shoots nestling together,
conforming to meet
within the round
of a bamboo basket,
and steam of heat.
One sure stroke.
Each moment
passing to
the next.

(Getting Galactic)

Somewhere in the center of the earth non-flightless birds are washing themselves in new dirt. Their full-spectrum songs spiraling upward, inward, to the core of their preening truth. Feathers, black, iridescent, green. Their center flight suspended outside the time-space pendulum of what is, what has been, and what will be. The present, imperfect past, future perfect past. *Yo sé. Ellos saben. Ellos saben bien.*

Yesterday I walked past your old house. The fence was falling down in the back. Center earth calling home the coursing of mineral songs. Signals perched, transmitting. The sag of a once-was-a-tree sighing home, returning. Your old house. The morphing container of this.

Bold piñata swinging gentle melody, empty slicing free. Moving anticipation to desire-crash through the gleam, sprinkling high-ground with brightly colored promise and seeds.

I walked past your old house yesterday. No one was home though there was a light on. Soft-burning amber rose glow. Central earth home. Going along seemingly alone. No one home, never alone. Wings breathing the breeze, so free. Quiet nest of strings, and buoyant fancy things, wrapped round to hold. Thin shells, future perfect, strength enough for new life and non-flightless birds. Preening truth. Born again, our collective inner spring.

(O)

the swell
the rise
the crest
the arc
the fall
the crash
the froth
the settling
the stillness
O

(The Ingenuity Shop)

And maybe we remember. Maybe we
remember what we learned as children about
walking the roadways at night and the importance
of wearing white. How, as fair knowing children,
we filled in the blanks saying to one another,
well, if we have nothing white to wear we'll
just strip down, leave our clothes in the
bushes beside the darkening road,
go naked instead.
Yeah.
Go Naked Instead.
Yeah.

Do Drive Slow.

(The Heat Is On)

Dear Anxiety,

It's been a while
since I wrote.
Still,
I think of you
everyday.

Water held round
in the belly of a
copper pitcher.
The permeability
of us questioned,
poured out,
poured over
the heart
of our certain
unfurling.

Bright middle-green
of a rising Christmas
tree farm
firmly rooted
in the July sun.

(The Fool)

If you stand on the edge of nothingness,
lips parted, eyes closed, and breathe in
deeply filling every question with recycled
hope, then exhale 'til you weep, you just
may start to feel you are. Yeah, if you
keep at it, elongating your release,
pressing your good belly into
the cradle of your spine,
you will,
curious
sigh,
find that,
yes...yes
you
are.

(Carpe Diem)

We can hold it, full, feel its weight in our hands,
spiny itchy pricks below strong spread of crown.
Imagining the sweet juicy trickle down.
Yeah.
We can turn it, sniff it,
gently chew it through time,
seeing, not seeing, the signals and signs.
Imagining what we will.

Our sometimes override.
Our dropping, slipping, our rolling wide.
Our bare humble stance.
Mud pressed feet
pausing together below heavy knees.
Carrying hard questions, bending the deep.
Here.
In the trickle down.
The ground of grown and growing.
Seeded, full, fed.

Sweeping forward to a kiss, to press our
clean noses and face our shared bliss.
Forever within us.
This.
In the receiving.
Our known unknowing.
Our scatter of bits enveloping
our madness,
our ankles, our zest.
Picking up again
to lay the table.
Smooth clean cloth
unfolding whole.
Pillows. Plumped.
Up.

(Holding On, Letting Go or So Much Bullshit)

How many times have I declared myself
to have crossed a line, to have evolved
into a new and positive way of being
from which I will never fall back?
How many times have I pulled this
threadbare trick from my shiny shiny
bag as if to offer myself
a crumb of control?
Many.
So many.
Security, assuredness, control....
So much bullshit.
Will I announce, once again, that I've crossed a line of no return?
I imagine I will.
There. No bullshit.
I'm reminded of a cup I had as a small child,
on it sat a small brown bear holding a cup
with a picture of a small brown bear holding a cup,
with a picture of a small brown bear holding a cup,
with a picture of a small brown bear holding a cup....
Oh, how I loved that cup.
It amazed me,
its going on forever.
Oh! This searching, this seeking, this
wanting to be free from our struggles
and limitations and all the ways we fool
ourselves into believing....
Sitting like a small brown bear.
Each of us holding our cup.
We fill it. Fill it. Fill it. Up.
Then in the end, we die.
No bullshit.

At the meditation retreat I cried in the shower.
I cried for so much bullshit. Raw and exposed,

feeling so close to something real and constant,
I let loose. I let loose for all my delusions,
all the games I play with myself, the tricks I
use to escape my sadness and confusion,
the polished imaginings I hold of
the self I wish to be.
"Abandon hope," they said.
A couple of weeks ago I found this so threatening.
"Abandon hope?" I said.
"What a terrible idea."
But today I get it.
I totally get it.
Hope takes us out from loving what is.
Sure, it can be visionary and creative.
I love hope.
Yet somehow it is false.
So much bullshit.

Yes. Abandon hope.

Freedom may be found each moment
as we live each moment as it is.
Sometimes we will get this
and sometimes we will not.
Sometimes I will be full of fear
to sing aloud before others
and sometimes I will say, "Fuck it,
who the fuck cares,"
and I will sing,
whole-heartedly
with total abandon,
butchering
and
beaming.

(Spelunking)

Moonlight casting through
the cave in the other room
countless miles away.
(If my heart
were
an alpine lake
I would dive, tired and naked,
pull its deep rubbery clay to shore
and smear myself laughing,
stretch my tender toes,
point to where I'd
come from. Point.
Flex.
Point. Flex.
Relax.)

(All Ears)

Without words we have
many things to say. Things
we've never heard before but,
can hear now wrapped in wind,
over and under, and breath steady
plenty. Wrapped in waves crashing
to punctuate new sentences. The rise.
The fall. The rise. The foamy whispers of
sincerity reaching out, creeping toward. And
sand caught in our cracks, itching to fall back
to allow us our open. As we know. No words
between. As we sit inside clouds of high silvery
gleam and travel this way and that without
collide. And while it may seem that some,
pale yellow fluff, are not moving, we are.
We, our most silent words, born of our
unspoken guts, our circling of liver,
deep filter of kidneys. Born of breath,
of heart, and millennium of spine.
Silently climbing our humble
throats to rest, momentarily,
on lips soft and parted.

(PSA)

Attention!
Mapmakers, seamstresses, onlookers, all....
Due to see through clouds and sticky
star-shining knots
we ask that you arm yourselves
with coral lanterns and rose oil,
stilts of cedar and warbler's song.
We ask that you make no sudden stops,
turn all old golden locks and open every box.
We ask that you return to
Grandma's turquoise overcoat, to
too big galoshes, red of hope
and knowing.

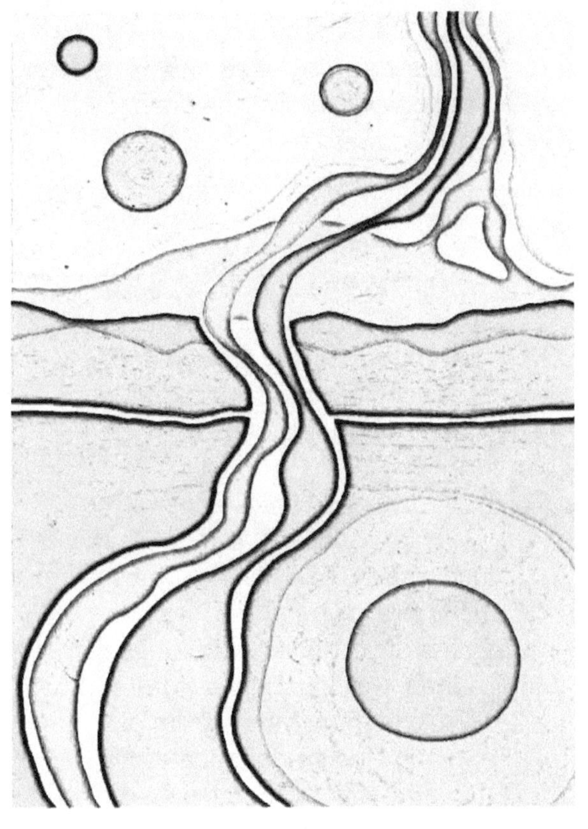

(Yes, No, Maybe So)

Dear Uncertainty,

Perhaps...
after sifting patiently through
smooth bulbs and hearty stalks,
round heavy heads
and bitter seeds,
closed flowers
and oblong fruits,
the dirt from
our nails scrubbed and
sliding away down the drain,
away toward new galaxies...
perhaps then, we'll....

Perhaps...
if I take you to dinner,
slip my shoes off under the table,
put my warm feet in your lap,
and ask you about your childhood...
perhaps then....

Or maybe, later,
at my house, if you
lean waaaay back laughing deep
and low, drawing me into the
timelessness of your most auspicious dance,
perhaps then, we'll finally know one another.
Trust in the erratic rhythm of
your wide swinging gate.

Yeah.
Maybe.

Perhaps.

(Place Your Order Here)

In the primordial void there is no buyer's remorse.
There is no "yesterday's gone", no frangipani scented
luau. Say it with me: "I am the primordial void." Say it
with me: "I am the primordial void." I know it can be
hard at times, like when we spill our grande double-
vanilla latte in the back floor-well of our car, extra
foam crashing atop Mount Everest, the beach at
Fiji. 12,000 travel brochures collected. Warm milky
promise tidal-pooling our new, moon-fiber
running shoes, puddling our flint and spark.
I know.
I know it can be hard.
I know...
this finger, here, at the end of a fumbling hand.
This pointy finger that loves to raise itself up...
extend outward with aghast aplomb, extend
accusation as if we are not the primordial void.

Damn!
I needed that latte.

Oh, heartbeat. Oh, empty bliss.

We, a damp, coffee-tinged, paper container
blowing winds of chaos, caught for a moment
in a leafless tree, returning to renew...
always,
all ways.

(Moonquake)

I was surprised this morning, arriving barefoot, naked, at the
beach, to find the sea frozen over. In an instant silver-blue salt
planes of waves lodging themselves high and low. From where I
stood. From where I stood. All movement ceased. Then you
arrived and did not speak. We climbed a dune. Crisp dry spray of
crystals suspending midair, suspending all we think. The
unexpected sting of tropical ice catching the river of our sleepy
throats, scratching new maps, new stories. New constellations
gulping down as breath, migrating fire. New galaxies orbiting new
centers within. Blinking ourselves open we look look look to the
sky, to our seemingly undercover shadow home. What's past,
what's new, linked and forever dancing, cloaked in rising light and
an evaporating sea to peel us back.

To peel us back on the spot.

Laughter.
Stars winking, "Yes."

"Yes, yes, yes."
"Hell, yes."

While heart shaped crabs crawl over our tentatively planted feet,
digging themselves translucent, funneling holes in warm, wet sand.
Going on about their day.

(Form Follows Function)

Imaging myself a chair
I do not care the time.
Legs shapely and
divine, I sit. I just sit.
In a corner. Open to
all that comes
my way.
After all,
knees
bend.

(Amanecer)

Deep in onyx land,
slumber-diving yield,
she lay outstretched,
bewitching herself
to the new day.
Tricking herself
away
from half-buried
truths-no-more.
Shadow core.
Covers sliding,
unheard, unnoticed,
from her long
serpentine wait.
Fog of two
great hands
upon her waist
she wakes.
Surprising herself
for all she is
already there.
As if
she could deny,
ever after,
the swan dive
of her divine,
curve of supple spine.
Slink of silken
treasure, her heartbeat's
forged feathers, her
molten fiery plume
of yes.
Oh, yes.
As if. All of this.
Yes.

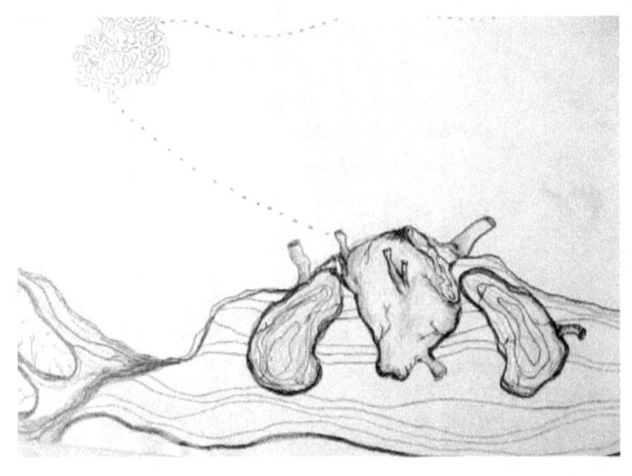

(Roots of Change)

Dear Impermanence,

I hope it's okay I borrowed
your shoes last night.
They're the perfect shade
of gray, though a little big.

When, in my cloud dress
I stood tall and child-smiled
into the garden mirror,
into the dry fragrant
smoke and dust of us,
I held my ground.

My perfect
momentary
ground.

Anyway...
eventually I
kicked those
nearly perfect
shoes
off
under a bush.
Flowering sundown.
Bright yellow awakening.
New moon reflection
projection connection.
And I danced,
glorious
and
barefoot,
upon the
rubble.

(For the Asking)

As the sun cracks the shade, purple and red, crystal formation,
sixteen hundred sweepings of endlessness and grace, the rain
plays a little trick instead. Instead, the rain, she reaches her clear-
blue satin palm down to broad leaves of clean, to stroke away
dark blocky outlines, our very-last trace of old and outgrown.

Renegade droplets springing quiet fire, alchemizing our tightness
and shame.

Fainter and fainter now, our cloud-heavy past transforms with the
spontaneity and humor of a slow-moving lavender rain.

And you, there.

You, there, in your little rowboat, painted a curling leaf, yellow-
gold, deep brown of earth and no return, I see you. You, there,
gliding within the open arms of a heart shaped lake, pulse of a
rising wake, quivering deep seeds, chirping tiny song, alighting
algae flame. You, there, rowing a brand-new scene.

I saved a place for you. That place you showed me last time
before our lungs had bloomed, bouquet of mystery not yet told.

You can moor your stealthy craft in my harbor, tie her up moon
strong and hop out to firming ground. Walk slowly toward the
place you know. The place you showed me, so I can show you.

~ *for Dusty Amor*

(Middle School Delight)

Serves 12
Preheat oven to 600°F

Proof in a large nest::

3 fresh ideas, seeded
2 cups dandelion fluff
1 first kiss
4 river stones

In a larger nest, sift and blend:

1 level cup good intentions
3 Tbsp. cream of desire
1 tsp. raw expectation
Pinch of shame
2 skinned knees

Add the contents of the
first nest to the second
in small handfuls, careful
not to gossip. Mix well.

Once it's smooth and free
of lumps, dump the mixture
upon a clean vanity mirror
and knead for 10 years.
If you happen to have a
mirror etched at the edge
with roses you may want
to add a tablespoon of salt.

Allow mixture to rise for 11
hours in a warm dark place.

Test it by turning on the
light and shouting,
"Meet me in the graveyard!"
If it falls allow it to rise
for another 11 hours.

Once stable, form into
a 13 foot braid and brush
thoroughly with a well
beaten recurrent dream
and dash of cool water.

Bake on a well-greased
platform for 10 more years.

Once cool, sprinkle with
freshly grated humility
and serve with fresh
sparrow tears, available
at many local track 'n fields.

Will keep
indefinitely
at 98.6°F.

(Once Upon a Time)

Don't despair, Buttercup.
Somewhere in your motley past an edible
violet once bright-eyed and sugar-crystaled atop
your eleventh-year birthday cake climbs delicate now
to ride upon a raft of childhood down. And with nary a sound,
no sweat on her brow, she floats wildflower assured.

To wash clean your pointed-elbow
smoke-screen scene. Your astral link.
To plunge deeply, shy smile.
Paper-dolls long holding hands.
Lips perched; candles blown.

She falls waterfall, (star light, star bright),
to align with yesterday's rose,
and deepest memories still to come.

Oh, don't despair, Buttercup.

Tho', if you do, please remember our
good tender roots and pedaling, fast
and furious, alone and uphill. New
school. Paper bag full o' candy,
a-swim of beads and salty pulls.
Slowing
yellow light.
The only thing weighing us down
as we pause to daisy chain, as we
dip our awkward awakening
to cool, clear the swirl of curdle
stew. Earthly atmosphere thinning
to hum a diamond shaped tune.

Endless and ever after.
Double dipped.

(Taking Flight)

This morning on my way to pay the electric bill two small amber-green birds flew across my path and landed beside a large seeping pool of silver-rose light at the four way stop. I looked all around, but couldn't find its source. A third bird, periwinkle with a citrine tail, joined the others and their conversation turned upward. I could barely make out what they were saying, but I believe it had something to do with a new material the smaller of the amber-green birds had discovered earlier near to where the late summer meadow meets the tributary. It sounded like the found-fluff had been buzzing, soft low-wailing, from the hollow of an ancient tree, and that she'd observed how this deep gentle sound of release was shaping the pull of the new string in her beak, pulling it back and in upon itself. This inner buzzing. Soft pulsing. Her tiny bird head, and neck, bright, and not knowing exactly what to do with such a font.

She said she'd show them, but she wasn't sure they'd see it, though it's always there, she said. Something about the stillness within the motion, she said.

Circling the pool of silver-rose light, which had grown by now to the size of a miniature lake, acting as if I had some great purpose so as not to tip off the birds. My shy curious eavesdropping. My too green faith. Suddenly a silent tune appeared. New waves of illumination, hot infinite truth, infusing the edges of the mysterious pool with ancient melody, my suspension guiding the cosmic ruse I knew I shared with the bright tiny birds. Softening the edges of my dry meadow mind. Slowing tempo, bending time. Pulling in, lyrical, new, to awaken unheard stillness. Nothing left to do.

Nothing left to do but drop my pale façade, to let fade stagnant rays. To dissolve my brittle pretend of ignorance and cool and to dive. To deep low-wail dive a new familiar bird, dive to the heart of the mysterious pool. Strip down. Take a feathery bath. Chirp and preen instead. Chirp and preen instead. Strip down.

(What She Said)

Dear Hubris,

Oh, I love you!

I love how you always
know just what to say.

And I love how you're always
here for me. The two of us heading
to the moon and back, invisible arms
linked, skipping our way to Thanksgiving
dinner, to the "Hell No!" demonstration at the
beach, to appeal that bullshit speeding ticket....

Oh, Hubris!

This morning when I lay
staring at your sleeping face
I saw a lot more lines around
your mouth. Deep channels and
moods worn of warring stories and
false solution. Yesterday's orbit spinning
conjunct to scepters and crusty borders,
dark centuries of pain. Oh, Hubris,
I love you so. The clean emerald
gleam in your eyes full of a knowing
all my own. All my own. My own.

All I own.

Own.
My own.

(My Tsunami)

Waking fresh, dew kissed, piqued,
in aqua green fields of old,
slippery woven sashes tying up night visions,
hanging them, suspended, from a giant crystal globe.
Lying back toes. Heaven immersed in
a wave of salted swirling.

"I was there once...", then returning.
And it was the same. And not the same.
Many worlds within worlds.
Dark reflective rivers flowing to meet and pool.
The sea, the back of my skull.
My tsunami.
My sensuality.

Thunder flash of insight.
Aching remembrance terraced high above it all.
Rocky mainstays and castle spires
tickling the backs
of naked thighs.

Opening closing eyes.

Hoping what lies the same, what has changed,
can be picked up, drawn up,
silver forked, rolled over,
mashed and chewed,
seventeen thousand
times.
Tasted eight hundred and four.
Swallowed seven.
Lost digestion found.
Infusing blood and body, my being,
with the ultimate
presence of peace.

(Scent of Sensibility)

Welcome.
Smooth sherbet sunset,
bursting notorious,
bursting hope,
Pacific
steely-blue,
orange-gray,
with waves,
as if
the full rising moon,
waxy-white,
yellow-green,
were not
already enough.

While softly,
below,
inside,
nostalgia glows upon the dial,
driving music, driving home,
Spanish ham,
warm winter toes.

(Return to Sender)

Dear Sorrow,

The other night when I crawled
through bright green brambles to settle
at your feet I had no idea you lived so
close. I thought I'd have to cross the
border, the border that's always closed.
I thought I'd have to carry a big umbrella,
two ply and tear streaked, for the distance.

So little do I know.
So little do I know.

The laughter of the blue-black birds
that led me to you also surprised me.
The crackling readiness of it. How it fell
from the lacework, veins of clouds and sky,
to pool at your open door. And start a fire.
When your dog came out to greet me
I reached toward her to scratch under
her invisible collar, but she turned away.
Her shadow erect, bipedal.
What's her name again?
Pandora?

I think it's great you don't rake
the fallen leaves up and suffocate
them in dark plastic bags.

Before I arrived I passed the
pagoda by the pond, kicking
a statue of a stone frog.
I had to hop the rest of the way.
By the end, I was on
my hands and knees.

My sheath of a polka dot
dress, torn, saturated. Abandoned.

Oh, Sorrow.
Did you know I was coming?
You homebody, you.

I thought I knew, but then, I didn't.

Climbing down the embankment my hair
kept falling into my unfamiliar face. The way
you pulled it back, so gently, smoothing my temples,
piling it up, releasing it, piling it up, brought new
light to the path, like little solar flares placed
along my spine.

I think I know.
Tho', I know I don't.

And it's okay.

As we smile together the cracks.
As we tend to stray dead branches.

(Expedia)

Sometimes our ghosts scare their see-through
selves, loose their sight and need to go on a
tropical beach vacation. Except when they live
at the tropical beach, then they head for Amsterdam.
Once they've booked their passage, they'll have little
trouble with the TSA, worrying not about having their
transparent palms brushed for poison, or if their carry-
on liquids exceed four ounces. These ghosts know.
These ghosts are one step ahead. Once they arrive,
they may wish they'd reserved a room at that other
place, the one closer to the arboretum, the one with
the gazebo and the lily pond, but they'll get over it
pretty quickly, and soon move on to turning back
beds and opening windows. After all, they have big
plans. It isn't very often they scare themselves into a
holiday, into seeing something new. It isn't very often
our hosty shadows check out. If they've timed it right,
they'll be able to take in the tulips, mile upon mile of
them in total bloom, wavering a rainbow sea. After a
couple days, they'll think about moving there, but
decide against it. After a week, they'll begin to miss
their work, but also to recognize that something in
them just isn't the same. That last scare, when they
looked in the mirror and saw a healthy pink glow of
cheeks and eyes a-sparkle with trust and glee reflected
back, well, that really took it out of 'em! Yeah, this trip
just isn't doing it, the northern coastal air too subtle
in its magic. Perhaps they're gonna have to book a
cruise of southern Italy. Visit Kerala. Patagonia. Havana.
Sublet their ancestral home. Cash in that ghosty 401K.

(Brand New Day)

I had a dream you and I
were making papier-mâché
dragons at that school I went
to when I was six, but then we
ran out of newspaper strips
and the dragons turned into
wooden ships and we climbed
aboard and sailed all the way
around the world. Granted
along the way the sun kept
setting and rising, setting
and rising. You and I holding
hands climbing in and out
of the boat, negotiating cool
rails, hot-warm sands, each
time, each time we touched
upon fresh familiar land.

(Shiver Me Timbers)

There are a few things that wash
a face clean every time. Absolutism
at its oxygen deprived best.
Continuous impress. Always,
all ways an inspired, "Yes!"

A few oceanic things that can
slide us way past, to cascade
our deep-yellow play, our sinking
sunlight floating dark-starry
blue to envelope us holy whole.

Yeah, even this. Dust-colored foam tickling
laughter, startled and slippery flee. Even this
can bring us to our knees. Honoring our
humble limits. Our long-hearted glee.

Strong shoulders squared to waves,
paddling arms to rise, to ride, to
twist the tide. Subside. Lean legs
looping twirls. Cool slink of hips.
Sweet glide.

New orbits.
Earth's rhythm true. This.
Absolutely.

Lost and found inside a soul's abyss,
a vibrational kiss cradled firmly within.
Warm, full-bodied-bliss.
New resonance.
Every surround. This.

Oh! To sing high to our wind-
tipped sky and wash our faces

clean. Wash our faces clean.
Every every time.

To sing it out fat,
a rat-a-tat-tat.
Fizz. Boom. Ba.
A rat-a-tat-tat.
There.
Take that!

Absolutely.

(ADDled)

Dear Distraction,

Like a rubber necking
siren whirling severed
vein blood spurting
you take me
from my oxygen.

And my neck is stiff.

(Hourglass)

There is this waiting,
between swells,
attentive,
active-passive.
This rising present
between shimmer shafts,
beaming down
our illumination.

La confianza.

Just above the horizon.

There is this seeping
through mist and clouds.
This reflecting ourselves.

Mar azul pálido.

Streaming possibility,
draining core intensity.
Uncertainty.
Floating atop,
we wait without.

Suspendido.

Half shadowed, half clear.
Mountains rappelling to meet
our feet. Motley stones rolling,
tumbling, jumping as if to say,
"This is it."

Todo eso.
Eso es.

Up upon the ridge,
feeling safe,
though crumbling,
a slow licking away of
old ideas, old foundations,
solid-ground bobbing us to
the top, to hallowed, to flight.
Igniting the pants of false gods.

Cada cabeza es un mundo.

¿Tú sabes?

If we dig deep enough
will it ever become dry again?

Does the crest that curls in
upon itself in transformation,
flatten to what's been
or
stretch
to
something
new?

Eso.

Eso es.

(I Do)

On the way to my wedding, overcast skies, rose bloom, I tripped, broke my toe, tearing the hem of my fair dress. And there at the curb, 7,026 figures spilled at my shrieking feet ripping a clamorous river tide, organza and gold, of all that was past, done and still to come. And I thought I might drown, had to put a stop to it. Yet no matter how I tried, stooped, prone, bent, squat, they simply would not pile up. These figures of mind just kept coming: spilling, pouring, roiling.

Uncertainty split at the seam on my wedding day.

Some were even driving trucks, axles hanging by a thread, taking wrong turns, almost as if on purpose. Very quickly I got to making tiny boxes, pulling from my storehouse and Saturn's wake, narrow streets of balsa wood. Nimbly cutting and fitting little cubes, one for each. Lifetime guarantee. "GOD is DOG backward." The boys at the back of the bus. Old Yeller. Stanley, my fourth-grade music teacher. My first boss. My first kiss. Off to see The Wizard. My festive funeral march. Fitting each gently inside and binding them up with a Tiffany blue ribbon I'd cut from the ever-changing sky. I had to be on time.

I took them to a fiery corner of the church and stacked them into a sandstone pyramid, my old cat Klem smiling silently on top, and I stood back. I stood back. One moment to the next. All tied up. Tight and neat. My trip, my fall contained. Contained in the boxes I had made and stacked up. *Ha Ha Ha*, but for the sound of jubilant laughter, golden rise of tide pulling free, and a pair of chubby scissor wielding hands. My innocent-self come to stay. Taking me down, box by box, cutting through what I thought I knew. What I planned. Warm hands constructing tiny splints from haphazard boxy streets, soft wood. Streets capable of flight when left to their own device. Wrapping splints with ivory seeded silk, round my shocked and smiling toes. Leading me to receive my first bite of cake. Ingredients, holy, unknown.

(And Repeat)

What To Do
When You Cannot
Tolerate Someone Else's Intolerance:
Laugh.
Laugh 'til you are coughing smoke,
then spit as faaaaaar as you can out a tiny window.
Spit again. Laugh. Cough deeply. Puke your rainbow
guts all over yourself. Clean it up with a picture of the
Intolerant One superimposed on your first baby blanket.
Laugh some more, laugh 'til you cry.
Spit.
Go silent.
Remember....
Laugh.
Spit.
Cry.
Puke again.
Laugh.
Kneel down.
Drop down.
Drop
your
self
down.

(Can I Ask You Something?)

What if we could turn
ourselves inside out?
Would we still want
to ride top toboggan
speed, dodging fragrant,
pop up trees?
Enjoy pressed duck,
éclade de moules,
mama sturgeon eggs
on a Parisian
New Year's Eve?
What if nowhere to go?
Nothing to prove?
All inside out.
Open heart,
stitches loose.
Coursing viscous
blue veined sleeves.
Would we want,
want, want
to climb
to the tippy
tippy top?
To the tippy top top,
no oxygen scene,
our teetering shadows
weak in the knees?
Über alles, after all is.
What if we stick
a finger in it?
Goo to center
what's real.
After all is.
Bumps
and quills

and spines
and stings
to sing from
the other side
of me to you, and
you to me.
Our armor crunched,
our combustible hunch,
our grid lock, Big Foot,
bramble hold punch.
What if we let go?
What if I saw you
and
you saw me
from the whole
of our holy other side?
What if I looked across
and got really, really lost?
Could you?
Wear my worn out
shoes? Swing back
from me, and me to you,
soft as newly
opened
eyes?

(Pocket o' Globe)

While I was standing in the garden listening to a conversation
between the morning glory of seeds, barely nicked and warm
waiting, and the philodendron in the upstairs bedroom, a crow
landed on an old drum head I use to scare away the birds. The
philodendron laughed breaking rhythm with the seeds. The seeds,
in turn, turned more deeply toward the trumpeting of the sun,
spilling themselves from the seashell shaped silver tray I balanced
at my waist.

The crow began to beat the wings of the drum. Feather fingerlings
of force announcing the coming of secrets, revealed, and space,
lungs full capacity. Announcing the shifting of decay. Soft yellow
light filled clouds, warm grassy slope. The laughter now of all, and
the seeds, now-gathering-now in my hand, unobserved, sweaty,
closed. Old-new sweet-dry seeds barely able to breathe.

The beating of the old broken drum. Tired heartbeat of what once
was. Rest in between. The interweaving of hope and slippery
means. And waves. Our birth. Our intricacies. Held close. Close. No
longer closed.

Fresh bright-green seams of laughter. Our opening. Shaker
maraca of light carved and clean. Ancestral nourishment. Dry soil
gleaned. Once more all possibility. Colliding to expand my old
sweaty hold. More and more. Space grown.

No longer extremities clinging control.
No longer extremities clinging control.

Pinky antenna, curl of thumb, moving along a tiny tickling bug.
Translucent river, soft wings, traversing eyelids never seen. New
gentle close. Seeds dropped to the ground. Darkness rolled.
Patted down. New gentle sniffing of things. Of the ever-cycling of
humus. Salt. Misty tourmaline. Gold.

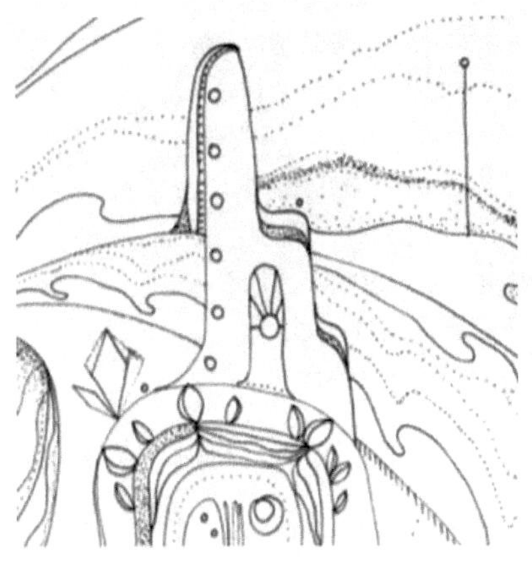

(The Other Cheek)

My Dear Compromise,

It looks like I missed my flight.
I won't be arriving until
tomorrow.
I can catch a lift if it's easier for you.
Waiting now at the rotating neon bar,
plate heaping "boneless chicken
wings", side of top shelf vodka.
Escaping my scruffy boots
and wonder.
Wondering again about the plans.
Do you think once we knock down the
low granite wall we could use the deep
gray stone to make a bridge to the
infinity
pool, toes barely touching?
And oh! I found an old leaded glass bird,
cobalt, emerald, gold, at the heritage
swap last week. Tripping ancestral.
I'm thinking it may be perfect for the
oculus
above the bed. Due to arrive Thursday.
Sorry, I have too much stuff,
and got caught up in customs.
Next time, I'll use *FedEx*, instead.
Thanks for keeping the light on.

(Reckoning)

If you wander all the cobbled, laundry-flight, back alleyways in search of the world's best pie you just may find it. It all depends.

On my way last week, neon-forest t-shirt flags, polka dotted bloomers and mismatched socks quilting our everyday sky, I passed a fruit and vegetable vendor dressed as a panda bear. She was practicing her tiny violin, while a well-dressed monkey, Versace, I think, scampered about rearranging the tomatoes, oranges, lemons, asparagus, yams and leeks into more and more complex, heaven reaching pyramids, a harvest of tomorrow's tombs and fertile temples, dark, fragrant river-streaming-barefoot and long robed passageways.

Mesmerized by the sight, I tripped over a loose stone and knocked a pink potato to the ground. After picking it up and taking the risk of placing it on top, I asked the bear if I might buy a basket of figs and she said, in what sounded like Japanese, No, two baskets. And so I did and she played a tiny Creole raga and sang to me, while the monkey balanced juicy shapes into a townhouse condo he saw in a magazine at the airport, just for fun. Spring onions method acting the foundation, life of a marble block, bouquets of lavender, sumac and thyme sprigging the urban roof top garden. I threw the biggest gold piece I had in my magic bean bag into his hat, a crimson beret he told me he'd inherited from his father's father's father's best friend, made of wool from the most ancient flock to scamper atop the rock of the Isle of No Man.

I asked them if they knew where I could find the best pie in all the world and whether or not it was savory or sweet? And they said Yes, I'd know it when I saw it, or maybe they said when I tasted it. Japanese sounds like Greek to me, which sounds a little like Portuguese. It may be around here, somewhere, the monkey said with a soft, low bow. It may not. And then the black and white bear broke a string on her egg sized violin and told me it was time for them to hang their laundry now.

(Twitterence)

Every day the birds begin
like a clattering of dishes being
put away high up on shelves
where small plants wade
in water roots swollen
with tall ideas.
Everyday
the birds
begin.
Circling in
as if it's never
been drawn before.
Spiraling our yellow
air as if in their
whirling and
chirping,
their long even tones,
they've not
said it all
before.

(Cake & Ice Cream)

Can we all just die a little?
Just a little?
Can we draw in
up and back from all
we believe we've created,
suspend ourselves above
our firmness of mapping?
Simply hover
awhile,
float down,
reach out to no thing.
Eggshell tentative fingertips.
Dagger sliding from the hip.
Cloud roar.
Yes
no
yes.
Wings beating gently back.
We die
and breathe.
Die to find
new openness,
new ways to navigate
the dark and viscous
drain and seep,
coursing clog of highways,
old and crusty thought.
Dull habit sliding from the hip.

Can we all just die a little?

Then come back.
Sing *Happy Birthday*
and really really
mean it.

(Pendulum Continuum)

Good morning, my heart.
Tight bud no longer.
Flowing lava upon
the breakfast table, and
a thickening of sky above.

Good morning, my heart.

As we climb from the cave,
casting Mars tinged glances.
Warriors throwing spears.
Flame of safety spilling
us across the dry plain,
burning green, purple, white.
Burning everything.
We run
with all our might
after and away
from our shadows.

Good morning, my heart.

Each day a walk about,
a shop about,
a solar panel saving, wind turbine
engraving slow down of despair.
Ice caps
split apart, two lungs,
transforming our wild fear.
Our tired impulse.
Kindergarten greed.
Confusion of need.

Good night, my heart.

The sun is setting,
no turning back,
no safety in numbers,
no discount rack.

Good night, my heart.

Into and of the sun.

No sudden stops to willingness.
Earth goes on with that.

Good night, my heart.
Earth goes on with that.
As a perfect snail,
translucent grain of hope,
tentacle left, feeling right,
circle waves through space
silently calling
our connection, slowly
seeding our grace.

(Puppet Master)

When waves rise up through
scrappy brown foam to bow
eternal azul take a long breath
then rise some more crashing
in-half to dash every piece of
all-we-could-ever-draw-up
upon a rocky pile of time
and my face is splashed,
eyes stinging with wakefulness
and warm laughing tears,
and
I-know-I-know-nothing lodges
under dirty-silver-moon nails
gently scratching the grit
of every trace we've ever met,
I scamper back down the rocks,
feet planting
to run,
to run
all-the-way back
as if pulled
by a glorious
raven winged
string.

(Last Call)

Dear Temptation,

Next time we meet I hope I
don't forget my glasses at home.
I really need them. And, oh! I'm so
glad you weren't wearing any scent.
You know how sensitive I am.

Thanks for the dance. Although I
wasn't that into the music it was
kind of cool to kick off my shoes
and let it take me where it wanted.
The crushed gravel was a bit
much, however,
pointed and hot.

Glad we stopped.

On my way walking home,
alone, crossing the dust
the detritus of something
old, something knew, I felt
the need to move from the
broken-hill sidewalk to the
wideness of uneven street,
but I didn't listen...just kept
climbing. Sliding my thin
crepe paper sole through
a smooth pile of shit.

At least
I didn't fall.
At least I
didn't fall
on my ass.

(Learning to Dive)

But then
I remember.
The sweetness
of remembering.
And I fold away
the string
of future intricacies.
Loose knit stitches.
I fold away the bulk.
Becoming fluid as a tadpole.
Imagining the deep
mud-bottomed pond
of my childhood.
With its spots of warm.
And spots of cool.
With its scum
and delicate webbing.
Rivulets clean.
Lily pads waxy
dark-blue-green.
It's teeming
streaming timelessness
of all that is unseen.
Tail a-swish.
Holding my breath
for a moment.
Blowing an eyelash.
Making a wish.

(We, Particle & Wave)

Tiny ribbons
streaming crystal
new beginnings.
The helix dance
budding deep inside
hard shelled seeds,
smiling upon darkness
and funky chaos
to reflect
patterns past,
suspended....
As once
we were water.
Rolling streaming roaring.
Rising to swell
beyond the banks,
beyond the aquifer,
over endless fields,
furrowed and clear,
to return again
to ripeness
and lunacy,
to return again
to sky.

(I'll Have What He's Having)

My friend told me on cold dreary days he goes alone to a honey lit café and orders two cappuccinos, one with extra foam. Then, he said, he leans across the worn table, leans in real close and tells his favorite joke, laughs out loud. Goes on. Smiles a lot. Leans in real close.

I suggested next time he bring a small round mirror, set himself up, really fall in love instead.

(Is There Gas in the Car?)

Remember that time we climbed the island volcano crawling
barefoot the sleek rock sided top, four fingers and a thumb
gripping life's little ledges, holding on and pulling up? Bowing to
the sun and dropping to our knees. You were wearing a crown I
think. Amethyst and gold. Or was that the bride from the other
party?

"Listen up, kids," someone said, "It's easy to get married. Hard to
stay that way."

Remember how we kissed inside the moon, wearing the shadow
of our collective whole? The klezmer satori wedding band ramping
up to overdrive, while the bride and the groom threw off their
black and white and got down on all fours, howling to seven
generations to come. And then your mortgage fell on your foot,
and for a second you were afraid your car would be towed, but
then a spotted owl swooped in with a bright green worm in her
beak, dropping to your shoulder, spinning raw silk round our tired,
creaky grid and I stopped breathing for a minute and you
smacked me gently on the ass. Then we fell down and the bride
fed us gluten-free Freedom Cake with a tiny platinum shovel and
the stars look very different today.

(In Consideration)

If the broom in the corner
could walk,
red peeling paint,
she just might choose
to sit down instead.
After all these years
silently teasing
cobwebs and silt,
tiny grains spilled
from wide mouthed
jars, slipping-large,
fast, eager hands.
She just might
put
her
feet
up.

(Divinity Fudge)

Salted caramel rolls melting
fingers sticky, licking clean
and grabbing a few seeded
words crunchy on the tongue.

For who knew?

Who knew it'd be you?

There
upon my
palm-potted doorstep
swaying a lop-sided
pajama breeze,
tickling my baby-blue dream.
Awakening my faith
in the bright unseen.

(New Collapse)

There was a Non-Festival in the plaza last night. The moon clear and half lit reflecting twelve rounds of sizzling wonder. Ooot million hidden faces. By the time my spirit hit the scene the horns of Heaven and Hell had been playing for eons. Waves of ever-sound climbing open walls to swirl the sky and settle, settle down to candlelit rooms, stacked kitchens, earthen holes.

My front door gets stuck a lot. I have to push out and pull in all at once to release its tight ancient lock. It took me a while to get out of my familiar, to trust the shift of shores, heed the call.

The street was rumbling with fire and hope, a crochet of smoke creating veils, dropping intricate weaves to our knees. Pale thinning smoke lifting the spirit revelers to the trees to sing high within thick branches of ease, of clean.

At the corner I met a buoyant silent soul who placed in my inward hand a satchel of magic seeds. I told her I thought I had some ideas for them. She "told" me I would first need to turn myself inside out.

I took the satchel to a dry quiet rise beneath the height of our illusion and sat down. The bag, raw and streaked, had been stitched with a tiny needle from the former USSR. Its weeping threads were easy to pull apart. Fragrant orange groves, deep crimson fields of clove, humble taro roots, purple potatoes, peanuts, corn. The satchel exhaling the crust and depth, ooot zillion faces murmuring non-promises of new light. The seeds inside alive and conspiring high.

With the last tiny pull of the threads three drops of warm salty blood fell to my head, my planted feet, as I brought a winged palm to the cave of my mouth and merged with ooot gillion years of void and trust. Well-being. As I swallowed the magic beans.

Soooon they shimmer-swoon danced for me. Then they laughed for me. And then they told me to run. Run, run, run. To plunge sweet river fingers into tight obsolete locks. To push out and pull in all at one. To recognize what is not.

(House of Mirrors)

Hello Restlessness,

I see you there,
in the kitchen, tying up
old strings and folding yourself
square. Egg white whipping frenzy
of promise and fill. Filling the layers.
Chocolate raspberry buttercream.
Because you can.
I see you, there,
in the hallway,
balancing the height,
straightening your view.

Again. I see you.

In the bath.
Plunging release
only a drain away.

There, in the study,
a verb of a room.

I. See. You.
I. Do. I. Do. I....

All the while,
checking, scrolling,
checking, scrolling.
Checking.
Scrolling.
Scrolling, scrolling. scrolling.
Just checking.
Resting less.
I do.

(Arches)

Under the covers
feet know everything
there is to know,
pointing gently,
this way and that,
they overlap,
bridge the gap
of busy itchy mind,
steady pooling
slippery thoughts,
rest into time.

(Strip Tease)

"Wear layers," we're advised,
thin and silky, woolly and crisp.
Slick. Beginning from our
rawest place we wrap
and smooth, cover
and shield, until our
winter sun,
our trust, returns.
Until comes a sign to
peel away the heavy overcoat,
to reveal, again, old tenderness.
Translucent insulation. Foggy
illusion. Ten-million-flavor
layers
in-between.
Peel. Them. Back.
One
by
one.
And laugh.
There.
Clean upon our back,
we unfurl....
What lies below,
warmed and worked with,
rising to the surface for sweet
breath. Purified by our whole
attention, our deepest ancient why
of presence and waking dreams.

(I Like to Run on the Beach)

What if they'd told me
upon first breath,
"Roll up your cuffs.
Hope bereft,"
would I have paused to cough?
Turned back to my bright, nearby,
ancestral star? Taken a spangled
flying car? Travelled through time
beyond and far? May. Be.
But, they waited instead.
Waited 'til I'd burned
sixteen layers of "Yes."
Sponge cake, velvet, marzipan, tulle,
sandstone, platinum, buckskin, cool,
paper-crete, cedarwood, coconut, stew,
helium, ocean, caterwaul, school. They knew.
Knew I did, too. And not a moment too soon.
So again, also "Yes,"
at thirty-two.
Red clay, sleepy rain, spider web, rope,
tortoise shell, onyx, beaver fur,
cope. Climbing high this box of soap.
One wide foot before the other.
One wide foot before the other.
Abandoning fear.
Abandoning hope.
Reaching toward that timeless goal.
Entrusting heart and golden soul.
Twelve octave cycle, tomorrow's slope.
Hot sand crunching suspicious toes.
Sweat clinging mind eyes and nose.
Flying high, bronze of arms, powerful
legs, cosmic heat, inner glow.
We flow.

Always our first breath...
evaporation every step.
One wide foot before the other.
What if they told me, forty-eight,
samsara, liquid, frenzy, grace.
What if they told me, what if they said,
"Abandon hope!" (Live instead.)
Abandon hope, live instead!

(Invitation)

Tell me your story,
the one where you fly
from crumb to crumb
a little brown finch pausing
to perch and preen upon
the sun of a window sill,
ten thousand feathers
ruffed
and opening.
If you tell me
I will listen,
really listen,
as the slow single streak,
of a tear upon a cheek,
overflows
with
your
release.

(Excavation Tune)

Dear Future Past,

It's true I left the light on for you.
Over my open doorway.
Pale blue memory
peeling back layers
of paint paint paint.
But, oh! I should have known
you'd use the back door.
That you'd shape-shift through
the rails and reptile piles,
the dust covered shade
and brittle articles
wired round
for safe keeping.
Ocean depths
of dumping.
In fact I did know.
But then
I didn't
want to
so I dug
a hole out
back, pretended
you surprised
me, instead.

(A Star Is Born)

This mountain,
magnetic,
raw,
seems unmoving,
but it is not.

(Pas de Deux)

Do you think the ice is solid?
That after many moons of slowing,
of waves of light contracting,
and expanding, contracting,
and expanding,
leathery leaves whirling,
and churning, whirling,
and churning,
water comes
to transform
in an instant?

This bridge
is here for us.

Ripples and crests
smoothed over.

Perhaps, we can walk it
together. You can
take my hand.
I'll be careful
not to slip and
pull you
down.
Though
if you'd rather,
we can skate.
Tie on slick blades,
do figure eights.
It may take some focus
to find our balance,
to trust a new flow,
but, once we do,
I'm sure

we can
glide.
I may want to take
the long way 'round.
And you?
I get the feeling you
may want to move fast.
Maybe cut through the rushes.
The edge is looking good to me.
I may even go backward,
leave the rugged shore
behind, practice
my strokes
on my own
for a while,
in between
creaks
and silence.
As if to say
there is
safety
in the
forgiveness
of vastness,
as if when
you ask me if
I know where I
come from, I think
for a moment I do not.

(Tea for Two)

Upon the great paneled door
comes a knock.

So gentle at first
I barely notice,
but I do,
I notice.
Inside my invisible guts.
Flip-flop.

I hear it.

Knock, knock.

Hugging close
my blustery soul.
All I think I already know.

Tho' I don't feel like getting up.

Oh, my painted egg shell.
Oh, my shallow harbor.

Again,
the knock.
This time more forceful,
emerald green with purpose,
splitting the air
with hoof beats,
ripe apples,
granite.

I look to the sky,
a-sparkle with emptiness,
sit up, and, reaching for the

sea across the table,
I yawn.

The wind bursts in,
all bells and gongs.
she will wait no more.

Steaming breath
upon my neck,
before an empty mirror.
Silently I see...
in her heavy cloak,
she is shaking and cold,
tired and worn,
streaked and torn,
rolled over
with deepest
valley boulders
and amber moss.
And she smiles at me.
And my muscles contract.
Relax.
Sure footed,
soft footed,
she goes to the stove,
puts the kettle on.
Copper flame a-blazing.
And
as the heat
reaches it's peak,
she streams before me
thickest, golden honey,
rounded hold of
silver spoon, and I
open my humbled self
to receive.

(Presently So)

Constantly becoming. We are. Magnificent green gold suns
orbiting moons of clean unseen. Expanding within. Deep centers
of heat and swirling presence. Our softness sidling through,
barefoot, to kick a small rough stone and hop up and down,
continue true. We are. The clean unseen. Sweet courage dancing
slow and close. Luminosity. And Grace. Scent of a rose. Smear of
chocolate across a wide-open face.

(Soapbox)

Yo, Self-righteous-nUs,

Comin' in here
all swagger and suede,
shooting your mouth off
slick as an Italian marble tile burn.
Cool blue smoke.

Well, of course we stand up,
of course, we take note.

Sensitive under skin
raising a blotchy red welt
from the inside out.

There must be a fire escape
around here somewhere.

(Unity Dam)

Dear Anxiety,

I've been wanting to write this letter for months, but I've been too busy trying to fix everything. Anyway, there's no more room for anymore of these letters in the box under my bed. This morning I saw a mini-jackalope in a black tulle pinafore fold up a few she'd pulled from the edge of the spilling box and form them into a wee boat, then, hop inside and sail off to China. Last week she'd tried digging there, but about three feet down she hit a giant root that connects the whole world and decided to accept this great tether and let it go, let go the hold she'd been digging digging digging for tomorrow.

Anyway, I was gonna write you, but my ear hurts.

Anyway, I've been meaning to write you, but then I had to take the garbage out. And do the recycling. On my way, the neighbor cat thumbed his nose at me and I tripped and fell down the stairs to Hell. On my birthday. I fell half way to Hell, but I felt really guilty about this and like maybe I'd curse myself. So I pretended I was falling up, up to Heaven, you know that place deep inside that we all are, but we forget all about cuz we're so busy trying to fix everything.

Dear Anxiety. Oh, my Dear Dear Anxiety.

Thanks for your amazing skillz. The way you move from the cha-cha to the Watusi to the mambo, tango, twist. Reel. Slow. It both confuses and inspires me. And I like this about life.

You know, if your chewing gum looses it's flavor on the bedpost overnight it's still there, you know? It doesn't make it lost.

I love you like a brother from another mother, you know that, too, right?

(Unzipped)

Like the brilliance
of a rising moon,
so clear,
so strong,
there on the horizon,
half hidden, half full,
penetrating, vibrating
sadness comes
dressed in a long
trailing gown,
itchy, gaudy, tight,
I unzip her.

(I Hear You)

I almost missed your call. The toilet was overflowing and the dog had just tore through the back door ripping the invisible screen seconds ahead of a swarm of killer bees which was fast approaching my bowed and sighing head. I tried to diffuse their charge with some nice smelling stuff to knock them off their path, not harm them. The only thing on hand, however, was a spray my mute neighbor had given me saying if used in combination with a talisman of the first love letter I ever received wrapped in my paternal grandmother's sigh of the setting sun and a peace of my son's first daughter's sleep the night before she bleeds, I could deliver the present of the future past.

I sprayed the potion at the onslaught.

The killer bees, like a midlife fire, rose to the star bit ceiling, roiling at first, then dispersed to sleepy couplets. Bzzzzzzz....

That's when I heard your call.

(Something Like This)

"Have you seen my gray shorts?"

"No.
Oh, you mean your *green* shorts?"

"No."

8 billion individual scenes
and an orange isn't orange.

Fuck it.
Let's go naked instead.

(Conscious Uncoupling)

Dear September,

What's happened?
Last year everything was golden bounty,
our equinoxal give and take satisfying
as warm apple pie á la mode at the lake,
bloom of lily pink sunset, sleep of loons.
Now you're roasting my tame swollen
heart, curling every hair from it's place
to middle outer space. I was so sure
you were the one, that you were the
best. Well, pretty sure.
Anyway, maybe it's not you.
Maybe it's me.
Maybe it's me
whose changed.
Do the cows, and clouds,
on the quieting-green hill
still smell the same after a
quick hard rain and black
currant tea with honey?
Could you be all we once
were without me?
Will I ever know
your sweet hold
of hope
again?

(True Story)

When I arrive I wonder if I'll be found out. I pace and growl this for a while, but then, the outline of a thousand fireflies softly humming from here to there within the sleep of the sun and a giant bamboo stand settles me to the moment. The Moment. This Eternal Moment...surrendering me like a rough lichen-traced cobblestone held within a salty earth once seeded and fresh. Shaping me a new road. I'm surprised, and also not surprised, curling my body to the ground, to the root of this explore, a perfect weave of fallen blade-shaped leaves, dusty, and half-way gone, or half-way home, depending upon one's current orbit. In a gentle effort to blend in I draw a transformation of leaves to my bare belly. Pull the pointy stick from beneath my back. Close my eyes to find a golden stream of tears. Our benevolence.

When she speaks to me of longing I place my hand upon my heart. And I breathe in. Everything. Half-way gone, or half-way home, depending upon one's orbit. A thousand silver arms of ancient tree applauding this courage. Tiny black and white dog scampering at our feet.

She says there are a ton of rocks in the little bay where I like to swim. "It's always this way at this time of year," she says, plucking an orange spotted bug from my hair and setting her free. Free to fly to the top of the sky, while we, she and I, shift our center in the hot dry sand.

"It's always this way."

True softness of unplanned trails reaching through tentative hold as I dive.

As I dive in. Head first.

Nary a rock to be seen.

(The Mystery Machine)

One precious frozen drop, vanilla ice cream, bonbons gobbled up
before the heat of wanton fingers can steal away the magic, cool
and dry. Sitting inside the open trunk, a veritable pirate's chest off
my chest. Superman cape and Scooby Doo mask, cascading
purple princess veils and wide gangster tie, a fedora once sat
upon and left way-up-high upon a shelf in the closet where the
heat of All-Talk gathers at the corners of a sly smile, a side of
cosmic swamp-flow stew.

I know it can be hard to relate to new.

I know it can be hard to perceive what we've never before
perceived.

I think costumes can help.

I think reels of palm size recording devices can help. Pretending
can help. Imagining something-the-fuck-else-until-it-is can help.
Pluto, Venus, Jupiter, Mars for the internal taking when we choose
the new, when we use our new words to change our new minds,
to grow our new faith in our basic goodness one day one day at a
time.

Scooby Dooby Dooooooo....

(Put It on Your Calendar)

My heart is a rainbow mountain.
Four chambers of Yes.
(And still I have to remind myself of this every day.)

(If a Tree Falls)

Whole-moon shadow-wrapping a
deep obsidian-blue blanket of perfect
death round our sleeping souls, inviting
our collective letting go, our spiritual
tending to splintered bones. Earth's daily
roll waking us, sandy eyed and buzzing.
Bare, barely poking-out toes balancing
our hold. Our willingness.
Cavern deep heartbeat.
Snowdrift to clear-running
stream. Tall stretch of
yellow yawning dream.
Incoming....
Thin light. And zest
of winter orange.
Frangipani bloom
just out of reach.
True reach....
Invisible
mosquito
sneaking
round.

(Reap What We Sow)

Dear Great Mystery,

   I made it to the Secret Garden! What an incredible place. Thank you for this timeless invitation. I feel so grateful and happy to be here. I was surprised, though, to find it so dry, yet overgrown.

   Last night under the eyes of a soft half-moon, I spent hours coaxing and clearing the "weeds" in the southern realms. Afterward I made a fire and burned them, along with my heavy outer garments. The flames purifying new ground. Oh! What a sight.

   Later, a doe and speckled fawn appeared from the East and told me stories of holy grace. Then I fell asleep in an owl's nest.

   When I awoke, the smoke had cleared, my skin wrapped still in the light of the moon. The sounds I heard reminding me of a black butterfly, wetness underfoot.

   I will not enter the density of the North today, but sun myself right here instead, right on the edge. Bare legs straddling two realms as one.

   Thank you, Forever and Always Infinite Mystery, for this open call to tend, to garden the secret-no-more.

(Deep Pockets)

Dear Melancholia,

I found the perfect hopscotch
rock for you, if you wanna come
over, meet me at the corner.
It's a flat white oval with
a vein of silver moving out.

Do you think we should jump
out of the box, scraped knees,
or spin and turn around,
spin and turn around,
before making our
way home again?

Do you still eat
your Oreos whole?

Deepest cosmos.
Dark matter.

Me, too.

Though I like to dunk.
Holding them under as long
as possible to absorb more,
to super-seep full with yielding.

Old friend, I found
the perfect rock.
You can have it.
I warmed it up
for you.

(After the Rain)

Dark wings, folded mostly, then fluttering
widening circles to unknown walls. Folded
mostly, to rest from ever rains, ever falling
air and sky dripping to collect in our biggest
chipped enamel pot dead center upon the
kitchen floor. Self-captive moth.
Folded mostly, to protect.
Cocoa brown eyes,
iridescent, powder kissed.
Deep wide ink-spot eyes.
Instinct, and quickness
of owls, blinking back in
questionable dance. To protect,
mostly, and then, too, to open.
To fly.
Passing by in a delicate
wobbly ellipse. To touch
a freshly bitten ankle and to say,
"Why, Hello! Yes. Here we
are out of sorts of sorts,
sky below, earth above."
Hanging peels of
ceiling, so ripe,
so long to sleep,
no sleep. This drip drip drip.
This inward season
of growth.

(I Love This Little Story)

As the rain came, quiet and yesterday, I was in the kitchen feeding the cats. The one with the mythically snakey tail had cornered a translucent baby gecko, while the wispy furred one circled them, closing in as if she were about to transform to flame. The sprinkling of the rain and the feeding brought us all back to center, but not before I spilled 223,000 individual pieces of kibble upon the sleek and streaky floor.

From the top of a heavy mango tree I heard a rainbow feathered bird say, "You know, you can sweep them all up into a tiny mountain and try to move it somewhere where it won't be disturbed, but it will never be new." I smiled. Crazy bird. Reading my mind again. I really need to stop feeding him all those question marks I find pushed up against the wall underneath the bed.

I swept up the pieces. I built them into a tiny tri-colored mountain of green fish, mini ochre planets and orange-red x's, but they wouldn't stay together. The x's kept sliding to the bottom and spilling forward, while the mini planets rolled toward all Four Corners. They were not listening to anything I had to say. I asked Mythically Snakey if she would help me, but she had just fallen, heavy head, into the pond after pondering her glorious stripey, spotted existence. She wanted only to sigh silently in Corner #3.

Wispy Fur said she'd help. She did so by eating all the green fish shaped bits. This was, indeed, a big help. She then slinked off to Corner #2.

Left with the ever rolling of the mini planets and the clattering of the orange-red x's I decided to name the place I stood Corner #5, then took out a tiny wooden flute and called, mellow and true, to the x's and o's, hugging and kissing myself for luck.

The smell of the rising sea was ripe in the warm wet air, the hair on my arms stood up as if a great clearing wind passed through. The tune of the flute came softly, echoing the rain and the sound of multiple heartbeats awakening from early morning emptiness.

The cats stirred, one stretching her back from a hunch of ready-haunches to a bow of open prayer. Rainbow Bird let rip a percussive wave of song, while the x's and o's lined up, one by one. The idea of the multiplex mountain, heaped and whole, snaking to new form, to new tendril allowance.

High order, and difference, allowing each to present and circle whole. Indifference left at the bottom of the pond, while the invisible, white and soft-brown spotted dog laughs with a trust never witnessed before.

(INFJP)

From my bubble I see everything.
Down through the buoyant wrap
of water wearing heat, knowing
not knowing....
Saw toothed peaks
ripping soft jade.
Scorpions hidden free,
diamond hiss and slink
at my invisible feet.
I see.

Everything.
From my bubble.

Gray blue silence of beating wings,
claws and crawls and caws.
Our being.
Our black-yellow dawn.

I see.

Hot pink
magenta aqua pine-green.
Jungle curtain's primal weave.

Over. Under.
Moon and sun.

Warping. Feeding ease.
Everything.

Tears of wind's ancient
tracking. Dousing. Waving.

As above...

so below.
Earthen bowl
laid full upon my lap.

I see.
Ribboning fields of maiz
pressed
between two coarse stones.

Heart shaped seeds
crushed to fruit,
fed wet
to dry paste
to steam.
Flattened between
ideas
lost
before they'd come.
Wrapped in husky
green.
I see.

Blind hands.
Eyes aglow, pyramid stones,
cut away holes.

I didn't see you for a minute.

You know when to go.

A thin white fog,
a smiling dog.
Floating coasting.
Waves. And arms.
Carried away,
with everything.
I see.

(Ice, Heat, Ice)

Crossing the highway to get to the other side I fell over an empty lane twisting my ankle, hopping in circles, stopping traffic. A red motorbike, pipes held to the belly with silver tape, swerved toward me in such a way that the person driving touched my outstretched arm, my balance, pulling me into a miracle.

Together, the driver and I fell to the hardness of fixed reality, tiny rocks pressing into the assurance of bones and flesh, yellow lines no longer dividing. And from here, we rolled, a soft sweeping "Ohhh", straight down the center of the endless road. By then, a patchwork crowd had gathered, calico, velvet, denim, silk...forming and dissolving edges, forming and dissolving, chanting their marvel up and down. Up then down. Up and down.

"Ooooohhhhh...."

While our "Ohhh", our sweeping, our magnificence, slow blurred slippery snake scales shedding, mouth to tail, beginning no end, rolled through the soul, gathering for a ten-point strike to break the surface and gasp. Our regeneration face up in the gutter beside a pool of cosmic light. Face up. The circling. Our dive. "Ohhhhhhh...."

The miracle of bruised palms and gritty knees rising together face to face to inner face the astonishment of our witnessing, twisted ankle turning round in relief of pain to create the miracle.

(Mappings)

Grace, known,
unknown.
Acting sometimes
as if it's all
already here.
And being correct.
Soft pieces born
and formed.
Invisible
networks.
Underground
fungus wrap
and snap.
Signals higher
than imagined.
Higher than
anticipated.
A true dog whistle is here.
New leather duckling
feet held to the
chest, held
through
to trace
the clean
of promise.

(Demitasse)

I see you, seeing me seeing you,
across the waving aisle, inside the midnight cool
of a swinging bench, inching the thin bright line
that wraps the tall buildings,
topping the vine-stitched cemetery where
everyone brushes themselves off
and sighs.
Seeing you seeing me.

Seeing you, and me seeing you seeing me,
though no eyes meet.

Though no eyes meet we sit across the table
communicating as stars, surges of speckled infinity
knocking the salt shaker to the next room.
The womb of a sugar bowl pitched
upside down to the tune of hallelujah.

Someone comes to take our order,
but it's already been placed.

Already known.

You as me, and me as We, bowing silently, noses to knees,
crowns to center earth.
Me seeing you seeing me seeing We,
linking elbows,
blowing course black pepper
to new tickling planes
of yes.

Thank you.

You Are Welcome.

Red Heart.

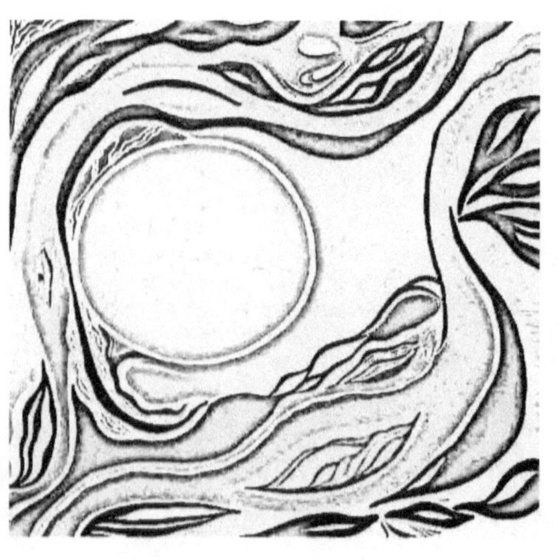

About the Author

Enza went to eight different schools by the time she was twelve. She used to feel proud to be such an easily adaptive human, and tho indeed to be adaptive is a part of her nature, and also something helpful, powerful and necessary, much of her capacity to adapt, and protect, as well as her general distrust in herself and others, was shaped from within a container of survival, insecurity and false identity.

At age thirteen her classmates voted her most talkative. At seventeen she was chosen class pessimist.

Several years after birthing her only child, at age forty, she came to believe in, and embrace, the basic goodness of humanity. What a game changer. She then consciously chose to shift her focus, to rewrite her cynical playbook and heal her human experience of distrust and separation.

Our minds are deeply powerful. For the most part we experience what we give our thought to. We are not our identity, opinions, nor preferences. Attuning more and more to her body, breath, and her unique and beautiful place in the grand scheme of things, Enza began to ground more and more into trust of herself and the unity and perfection of all. Our benevolence. Sharing her vision in words and images is her way of honoring her uniqueness, gratitude and faith. *Thank you.*

This is her second book of drawings, poems & stories.

It is with great pleasure
I share with you
my curiosity and
creative expression.

My website has pages for all: murals, paintings, Open
Stage events, poetry, books, song, art for art's sake and
heartfelt encouragement.

www.deeplowbow.com

www.ingramcontent.com/pod-product-compliance
Lightning Source LLC
Chambersburg PA
CBHW022007170726
47994CB00023B/2417